GUITAR · VOCAL

THE GREATEST SHOWMAN
MUSIC FROM THE MOTION PICTURE SOUNDTRACK

ISBN: 978-1-5400-2966-9

Visit Hal Leonard Online at
www.halleonard.com

Contact Us:
Hal Leonard
7777 West Bluemound Road
Milwaukee, WI 53213
Email: info@halleonard.com

In Europe contact:
Hal Leonard Europe Limited
Distribution Centre, Newmarket Road
Bury St Edmunds, Suffolk, IP33 3YB
Email: info@halleonardeurope.com

In Australia contact:
Hal Leonard Australia Pty. Ltd.
4 Lentara Court
Cheltenham, Victoria, 3192 Australia
Email: info@halleonard.com.au

4
THE GREATEST SHOW

8
A MILLION DREAMS

12
COME ALIVE

16
THE OTHER SIDE

21
NEVER ENOUGH

24
THIS IS ME

28
REWRITE THE STARS

32
TIGHTROPE

35
FROM NOW ON

The Greatest Show

Words and Music by Benj Pasek,
Justin Paul and Ryan Lewis

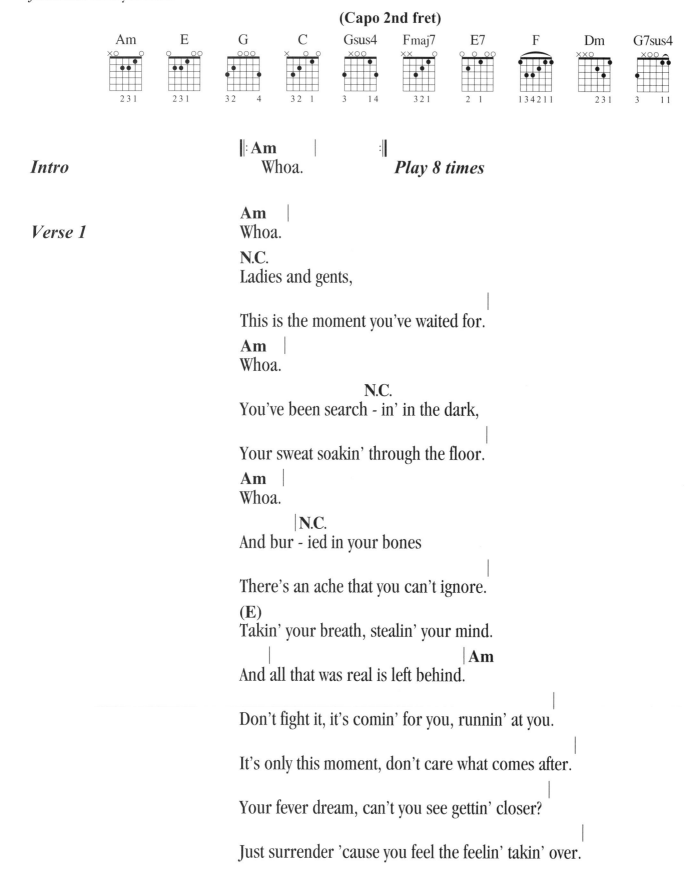

(Capo 2nd fret)

Am   E   G   C   Gsus4   Fmaj7   E7   F   Dm   G7sus4

Intro

‖: **Am** | :‖
Whoa.   ***Play 8 times***

Verse 1

Am |
Whoa.

N.C.
Ladies and gents,

|
This is the moment you've waited for.
Am |
Whoa.

N.C.
You've been search - in' in the dark,

|
Your sweat soakin' through the floor.
Am |
Whoa.

|**N.C.**
And bur - ied in your bones

|
There's an ache that you can't ignore.
(E)
Takin' your breath, stealin' your mind.
| |**Am**
And all that was real is left behind.

|
Don't fight it, it's comin' for you, runnin' at you.

|
It's only this moment, don't care what comes after.

|
Your fever dream, can't you see gettin' closer?

|
Just surrender 'cause you feel the feelin' takin' over.

|
It's fire, it's freedom, it's floodin' open.

|
It's a preacher in the pulpit and your blind devotion.

There's somethin' breakin' at the brick of ev'ry wall
        |E
That's holdin' all that you know.
  G N.C.   ‖
So tell me, do you wanna go…

Chorus 1

C   Gsus4 |Am
Where it's cov - ered in all the colored lights?
          Fmaj7 |C
Where the run - aways are runnin' the night
              E7 |Am
Impossible comes ____ true. It's takin' o - ver you.
    F |C
Oh! This is the greatest show!
  Gsus4 |Am
We light it up, we won't come down.
       Fmaj7 |C
And the sun ____ can't stop us now.
           E7 |Am
Watchin' it come ____ true, it's takin' o - ver you. Oh!
F |C   ‖
This is the greatest show!

Verse 2

Am |
Whoa.

  | |
Co - lossal we come, these renegades in the ring.
F
Whoa.
         |Dm
Where the lost ____ get found
        E |Am
And we crown ____ 'em the circus kings.
                    |
Don't fight it, is comin' for you, runnin' at you.

                    |
It's only this moment, don't care what comes after.
                 |
It's blindin', outshinin' anything that you know.
          F   N.C.   ‖
Just surrender 'cause you're comin' and you wanna go…

Chorus 2

C   Gsus4 |Am
    Where it's cov - ered in all the colored lights?

        Fmaj7 |C
Where the run - aways are runnin' the night

           E7 |Am
Impossible comes ___ true. Intoxica - tin' you.

    F |C
Oh! This is the greatest show!

    Gsus4 |Am
We light it up, we won't come down.

      Fmaj7 |C
And the sun ___ can't stop us now.

          E7 |Am
Watchin' it come ___ true, it's takin' o - ver you. Oh!

F   ‖Am
This is the greatest show!

Bridge

Am |F
    It's ev'rything you ever want.

           |C
It's ev'rything you ever need.

             |G
And it's here, right in front of you.

                    |Am
(This is where you...) This is where you wanna be.

      |F
It's ev'rything you ever want.

      |C
It's ev'rything you ever need.

          |G
And it's here, right in front of you.

         G7sus4 |
This is where you wanna be.

N.C.
This is where you wanna be.

Chorus 3   *Repeat Chorus 1*

Outro-Chorus

    C   Gsus4 |Am
Where it's cov - ered in all the covered lights?

                        F |C
Where the run - aways are runnin' the night.

                     E7 |Am
Impossible comes ___ true. It's takin' o - ver you.

     F |C
Oh! This is the greatest show!

    Gsus4 |Am
We light it up, we won't come down.

                F |C
And the walls ___ can't stop us now.

                    E7 |Am
Watchin' it come ___ true, it's takin' o - ver you.

     F |
Oh! This is the greatest...

C   Gsus4
Yes, ev'rything you want is right in front   of you.
Show!

         |Am   F
And you see   the impossible is coming true,

               |C   Gsus4 |Am
And the walls ___ can't stop us now.

F |
This is the greatest...

‖:C
   Show! Oh!

Gsus4   Am
This is the greatest show!

    F   :‖
Oh! This is the greatest...   _**Play 4 times**_

C | ‖
Show!

A Million Dreams

Words and Music by
Benj Pasek and Justin Paul

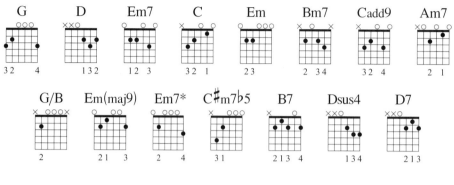

Intro

|G |D |Em7 |C |

|G |D |C | ||

Verse 1

G |D |Em7

I close my eyes ___ and I can see

                    |C |G |D |C | |G

A world that's wait - ing up for me ___ that I call my own.

                    |D |Em7

Through the dark, ___ through the door,

                    |C |G

Through were no ___ one's been before,

|D |C | ||

But it feels like home.

Pre-Chorus 1

D |Em   Bm7 |Cadd9 | |D

They can say, they can say it all ___ sounds crazy.

                    |Em   Bm7 |C |Am7 |D

They can say, they can say I've lost ___ my mind.

                    |Em   Bm7 |Cadd9 | |Bm7

I don't care, I don't care, so call me crazy.

                    |Em   Bm7 |Cadd9 |

We can live in a world that we ___ design.

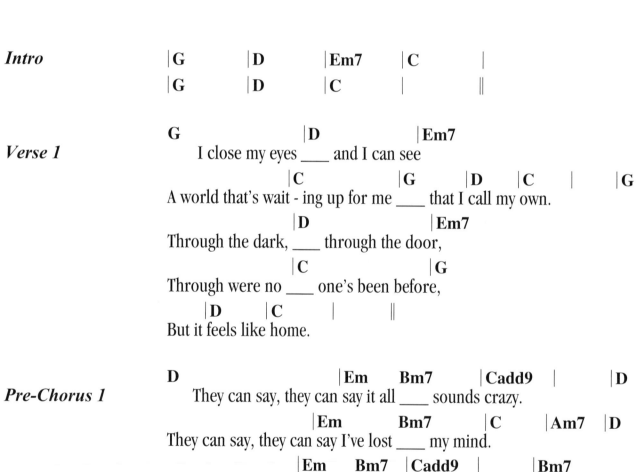

Chorus 1

```
          ‖G              |
'Cause ev'ry night I lie  in bed,
       |D                 |
The brightest colors fill  my head.
    |Am7              |        G/B    |C          |
A million dreams are keep - in' me ___ awake.
    |G                    |
I  think of what the world  could be,
    |D                |
A vision of the one  I see.
    |Am7              |   G/B    |C        |Cadd9
A million dreams is all  it's gonna take.
        |N.C.                  |                        ‖
Oh, a million dreams for the world we're gonna make.
```

Interlude 1

```
|G          |D          |Em7        |C          ‖
```

Verse 2

```
G                       |D            |Em7
   There's a house ___ we can build,
            |C            |G  |D           |C     |   |G
Ev'ry room ___ inside is filled ___ with things from far away.
                |D       |Em7
Special things ___ I compile,
              |C                  |G        |
Each one there ___ to make you smile
      D   |C       |       ‖
On a rainy day.
```

Pre-Chorus 2

```
D                          |Em    Bm7      |Cadd9  |        |D
   They can say, they can say it all ___ sounds crazy.
                        |Em      Bm7      |C    |Am7  |D
They can say, they can say we've lost ___ our minds.
                      |Em       Bm7 |Cadd9   |      |Bm7
I don't care, I don't care, if they call us crazy.
                     |Em       Bm7    |C       |Cadd9
Run away to a world that we ___ design.
```

Chorus 2   *Repeat Chorus 1*

Interlude 2
G	D	Am7	
G	D	Em	C
C	|D		

Chorus 3
G |
Ev'ry night I lie in bed,
 |D |
The brightest colors fill my head.
 |Am7 | G/B |C |
A million dreams are keep - in' me ___ awake.
 |G |
I think of what the world could be,
 |D |
A vision of the one I see.
 |Am7 | G/B |C |Cadd9
A million dreams is all it's gonna take.
 |N.C. | ||
Oh, a million dreams for the world we're gonna make.

Bridge
Em |Em(maj9) |Em7*
 However big, ___ however small,
 |C#m7♭5 |Cadd9 |
Let me be part of it all.
 |G | B7 |Em
Share your dreams ___ with me.
 |Em(maj9) |Em7*
You may be right, ___ you may be wrong,
 |C#m7♭5 |Am7 | |G/B
But say that you'll bring me along ___ to the world you see.
 | |Cadd9 |C
To the world I close my eyes to see,
 |Dsus4 |D7 |
I close my eyes to see.

Chorus 4

```
       ‖G                    |
'Cause  ev'ry night I lie in bed
        |D                   |
The brightest colors fill my head.
       |Am7                |           |C
A million dreams are keep - in' me awake.
        |                  |
A million dreams, a mil - lion dreams.
       |G                   |
I think of what the world  could be,
       |D                |
A vision of the one  I see.
        |Am7              |  G/B     |C          |
A million dreams is all it's gonna take.
        |                 |                  |G      |D     |Em7* |
A  million dreams for the world we're gonna make,
Cadd9      |                       |G      |D      |Cadd9  ‖
   For the world we're gonna make.
```

Come Alive

Words and Music by
Benj Pasek and Justin Paul

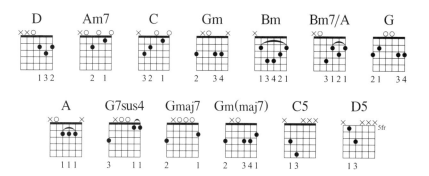

Verse 1

  D |**Am7** |**C**
You stumble through your days, got your head hung low,

|**Gm** |**D**
Your sky's a shade of grey.

              |**Am7** |**C**
Like a zombie in a maze, you're a - sleep inside,

|**Gm** ||
But you can shake awake.

Pre-Chorus 1

Bm |**Bm7/A**
    'Cause you're just a dead man walkin',

                    |**G**
Thinkin' that's your only option.

But you can flip the switch
| **A**   **Bm**|
And brighten up your dark - est day.

                  |**Bm7/A**
Sun is up and the color's blindin'.

                |**G7sus4**
Take a world and redefine it.

Leave behind your narrow mind.
| **N.C.**
You'll never be the same.

Chorus 1

       ‖**D** |**Am7**

Come alive, ___ come alive.

      |**Gmaj7**

Go and light ___ your light.

      |**Gm(maj7)**

Let it burn ___ so bright.

       |**D** |**Am7**

Reachin' up ___ to the sky,

      |**Gmaj7**

And it's o - pen wide.

      |**Gm(maj7)**   N.C.

You're elec - trified.

Bridge 1

      ‖**D**

And the world becomes a fantasy,

      |**Am7**

And you're more than you could ever be,

      |**C** |**G**

'Cause you're dreamin' with your eyes wide open

      |**D**

And you know you can't go back again

     |**Am7**

To the world that you were livin' in,

      |**C** |**G**

'Cause you're dreamin' with your eyes wide open.

      ‖

So come alive!

Interlude 1

|**C5** **D5** N.C. | **C5** |**D5** N.C. | ‖

Verse 2

D |**Am7**

  I see it in your eyes,

     |**C** |**Gm** |**D**

You be - lieve that lie that you need to hide your face.

         |**Am7** |**C**

Afraid to step out - side so you lock the door.

   |**Gm**   ‖

But don't you stay that way.

Pre-Chorus 2

   Bm |**Bm7/A**
No more livin' in those shadows.

                                |**G**
You and me, we know how that goes.

'Cause once you see it,

           | **A   Bm**|
Oh, you'll never, never be the same.

                  |**Bm7/A**
A little bit of lightnin' strikin',

                  |**G7sus4**
Bottled up to keep on shinin'.

You can prove there's more to you.

   | **N.C.** ‖
You cannot be afraid.

Chorus 2   *Repeat Chorus 1*

Bridge 2

          ‖**D**
And the world becomes a fantasy,

           |**Am7**
And you're more than you could ever be,

             |**C** |**G**
'Cause you're dreamin' with your eyes wide open

          |**D**
And we know we can't go back again

          |**Am7**
To the world that we were livin' in,

             |**C** |**G**
'Cause we're dreamin' with our eyes wide open.

           ‖
So come alive!

Interlude 2 |**D5** **N.C.**   ‖:**D5**   :‖ *Play 9 times*

Breakdown

N.C. | |
Come one, come all, come in, come on.

          | |
To anyone who's bursting with a dream.

          | |
Come one, come all, you hear the call.

         | | **C**
To anyone who's searchin' for a way to break free.

   | **G** |
Break free. Break free.

Bridge 3

       ‖ **D**
And the world becomes a fantasy,

     | **Am7**
And you're more than you could ever be,

     | **C** | **G**
'Cause you're dreamin' with your eyes wide open

    | **D**
And we know we can't go back again

   | **Am7**
To the world that we were livin' in,

     | **C** | **G**   **N.C.**
'Cause we're dreamin' with our eyes wide open.

   | **D**
And the world becomes a fantasy,

     | **Am7**
And you're more than you could ever be,

   | **C** | **G**
'Cause you're dreamin' with your eyes wide open

   | **D**
And we know we can't go back again

   | **Am7**
To the world that we were livin' in,

   | **C** | **G**
'Cause we're dreamin' with our eyes wide open.

   | **C** | **G**
'Cause we're dreamin' with our eyes wide open.

N.C. | **D**   ‖
So come alive!

The Other Side

Words and Music by
Benj Pasek and Justin Paul

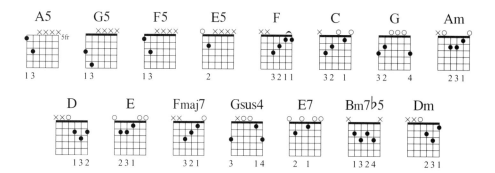

Intro |**A5** |**G5** |**F5** |**E5 N.C.** ||

Verse 1

A5 |**G5** |**F5**
     Right here, right now,   I put the offer out.
                                                              |**E5   N.C.** |
I don't wanna chase you down, I know you see it.
A5 |**G5** |**F5**
     You run with me   and I can cut you free,
                                              |**E5   N.C.** | |
Out of the drudgery and walls you keep in.
F |**C** |**G**
     So trade your typical   for somethin' colorful,
                              |**Am**   **G** |
And if it's crazy, live a little crazy.
F |**C** |**D**
     You can play it sensible, a king of conventional,
                              |**E** | **N.C.** ||
Or you can risk it all and see.

Chorus 1

Fmaj7 |C
Don't you wanna get away

    |G |Am
From the same old part you gotta play?

     |Fmaj7 |C |Gsus4
'Cause I got what you need, so come ___ with me and take the ride,

     |Am   Gsus4 |F
It'll take you to the other side.

                             |C |G
'Cause you can do like you do   or you can do like me.

              |Am   Gsus4 |
Stay in the cage, or you finally take   the key.

Fmaj7 |C |Gsus4
Oh damn, suddenly you're free to fly.

      |E7   ‖
It'll take you to the other side.

Verse 2

A5 |G5 |F5
   Okay, my friend,   you wanna cut me in?

                       |E5 N.C. |
Well, I hate to tell you, but it just won't happen.

A5 |G5 |F5
   So thanks, but no,   I think I'm good to go.

            |E5 N.C. | |
I quite enjoy the life you say   I'm trapped in.

F |C |G
   Now I admire you   and that whole show you do.

              |Am   G |
You're onto somethin'. Really, it's somethin'.

F |C |D
   But I live among the swells and we don't pick up peanut shells.

                    |E   ‖
I'll have to leave that up to you.

Chorus 2

Fmaj7 |**C**
Don't you know that I am okay

    |**G** |**Am**
With this uptown part I get to play?

    |**Fmaj7** |**C** |**Gsus4**
'Cause I got what I need, and I ___ don't wanna take the ride.

             |**Am** **Gsus4** |**F**
I don't need to see the other side.

                           |**C** |**G**
So go and do like you do.   I'm good to do like me.

                |**Am**   **Gsus4** |
Ain't in a cage, so I don't need to take ___ the key.

Fmaj7 |**C** |**Gsus4**
Oh damn, can't you see I'm doing fine?

             |**E7**
I don't need to see the other side.

Bridge

      ||**F** |**C**
Now, is this really how you'd like to spend your days?

  |**G** |**Am**   **G**
Whis - key and misery and parties and plays.

        |**F** |**C**
If I were mixed up with you, I'd be the talk of the town;

        |**G** |**E7**
Disgraced ___ and disowned, another one of the clowns.

         |**F** |**C** |**G**
But you would finally live a little, ___ fin'lly laugh a little.

               |**Am**   **G**
Just let me give you the free - dom to dream

        |**F** |**C** |**D**
And it'll wake you up and cure your achin'

                | |**Fmaj7**
Take your walls and start 'em breakin',

                  | |**Bm7♭5**
Now that's a deal that seems worth takin'

                  |**E7** ||
But I guess I'll leave that up to you.

Pre-Chorus

Am | |
     Well, it's intriguing, but to go would cost me greatly.

          | |**Dm**
So what percentage of the show would I be taking?

             | |**Am**
Well, fair enough, you'd want a piece of all the action.

          | |**E7**
I'd give you seven. We could shake and make it happen.

          | |**F**
I wasn't born this morning. Eighteen would be just fine.

          | |**E7**
Why not just go ahead and ask for nickels on the dime?

Fifteen.

   |**F**
I'd do eight.

Twelve.

    |
Maybe nine.

E7   N.C. | ‖
Ten!

Fmaj7 |C
Don't you wanna get away

  |G |Am
To a whole new part you're gonna play?

     |Fmaj7
'Cause I got what you need,

    |C |Gsus4 |
So come ___ with me and take the ride

Am   **Gsus4** |F
To the other side.

             |C
So if you do like I do,...

                |G
So if you do like me,...

Forget the cage

     |Am   Gsus4 |
'Cause we know how to make   the key.

Fmaj7 |C |Gsus4
Oh damn, suddenly we're free to fly.

      |Am   **Gsus4** |
We're goin' to the other…

F |
Side. (So if you do like I do,)

C |Gsus4
To the other side.   (So if you do like me,)

   |Am   **Gsus4** |F
Goin' to the other side.

                   |
('Cause if you do, we goin'…)

C |Gsus4
To the other side,

     |E7 |N.C.   ‖
We're goin' to the other side.

Never Enough

Words and Music by
Benj Pasek and Justin Paul

(Capo 1st fret)

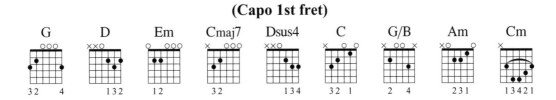

Intro

|G   D |Em |G   D |Em ||

Verse 1

      G   D |Em
    I'm tryin' to hold my breath.

    |Cmaj7 G
Let it stay this way.

    |Dsus4 D |G
Can't let this   moment end.

              D |Em
You set off a dream in me.

    |Cmaj7   G
Gettin' louder now.

    |Dsus4 |Em
Can you hear it echoing?

             |C
Take my hand.

                 |G/B
Will you share this with me?

                |Dsus4 D ||
'Cause darling, with - out you,

Chorus 1

```
                     G                                    |D
                          All the shine of a thousand spotlights,

                     All the stars we steal from the night sky
                          |Am        Em    |C                    |
                     Will never be e - nough, never be enough.
                     G
                     Towers of gold are still too little.
                          |D
                     These hands could hold the world,
                          |Am           Em    |
                     But it'll never be e - nough,
                     C            |                |G
                     Never be e - nough for me.
                                  |D              |Em
                     Never, never,     never, never,
                                  |C           |
                     Never for me, ___ for me.
                     G          |D             |
                     Never enough, never enough,
                     Em                    |C
                     Never enough for me, ___ for me.
                              |        ‖
                     For me,
```

Chorus 2

G |D

All the shine of a thousand spotlights,

All the stars we steal from the night sky
   |Am   Em |C |
Will never be e - nough, never be enough.

G
Towers of gold are still too little.
     |D
These hands could hold the world,
       |Am   Em |
But it'll never be e - nough,

C | Cm |G
Never be e - nough ___ for me.
                |D |Em
Never, never,   never, never,
              |C |
Never for me, ___ for me.

G |
Never enough, never, never.

D |
Never enough, never, never.

Em |C
Never enough for me, ___ for me.
       | |N.C. | G   ‖
For me,   for me.

This Is Me

Words and Music by
Benj Pasek and Justin Paul

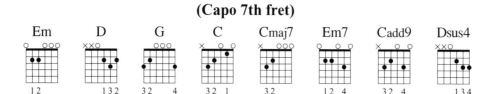

(Capo 7th fret)

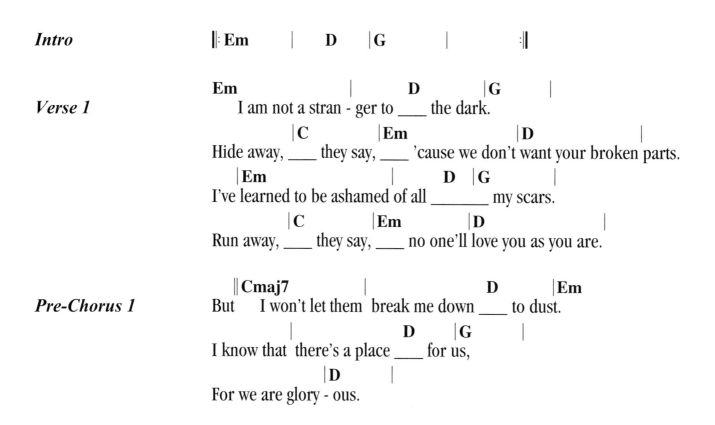

Intro ‖: Em | D |G | :‖

Verse 1

Em | D |G |
     I am not a stran - ger to ___ the dark.
           |C |Em |D |
Hide away, ___ they say, ___ 'cause we don't want your broken parts.
       |Em | D |G |
I've learned to be ashamed of all _____ my scars.
       |C |Em |D |
Run away, ___ they say, ___ no one'll love you as you are.

Pre-Chorus 1

    ‖Cmaj7 | D |Em
But   I won't let them break me down ___ to dust.
           | D |G |
I know that there's a place ___ for us,
           |D |
For we are glory - ous.

Chorus 1

‖ **G** | | |
When the sharpest words wanna cut me down,

|**Em7** | | |
I'm gonna send a flood, gonna drown 'em out.

|**Cadd9** |
I am brave,   I am bruised.

|**Dsus4** |**N.C.**
I am who ___ I'm meant to be.

|**G**
This is me.

                     | | |
Look out, 'cause here I come;

|**Em7** | | |
And I'm marchin' on to the beat I drum.

      |**Cadd9** | |**Dsus4** |**N.C.**
I'm not scared   to be seen. I make no ___ apologies.

      ‖
This is me.

Interlude 1

    G | | | **D** |
(Oh.   Oh.

Em | | | |**Cadd9**
Oh.   Oh.   Oh.

    | |**D** |**N.C.**
Oh.   Oh.   Oh, oh.)

Verse 2

```
     ‖Em          |          D    |G          |
```
An - other round of bullets hits my skin.
```
                    |C          |Em      |D                    |
```
Well, fire away, ___ 'cause to - day I won't let the shame sink in.
```
     |Em          |          D    |G          |
```
We are burstin' through the barricades ___ and reachin' for the sun.
```
     |C        |Em    |D                    |          ‖
```
(We are warriors.) ___ Yeah, that's what we've become.

Pre-Chorus 2

```
Cmaj7          |          D        |Em
```
    I won't let them break me down ___ to dust.
```
          |          D    |G          |
```
I know that there's a place ___ for us,
```
          C    |D  N.C.    |
```
For we are glo - rious.

Chorus 2

```
          ‖G          |          |          |     D
```
When the sharpest words wanna cut me down,
```
          |Em7          |          |          |
```
I'm gonna send a flood, gonna drown 'em out.
```
          |Cadd9          |
```
I am brave,   I am bruised.
```
          |Dsus4          |N.C.
```
I am who ___ I'm meant to be.
```
          |G
```
This is me.

```
          |          |          |
```
Look out, 'cause here I come;
```
          |Em7          |          |          |
```
And I'm marchin' on to the beat I drum.
```
          |Cadd9          |          |Dsus4          |N.C.
```
I'm not scared   to be seen. I make no ___ apologies.
```
          ‖
```
This is me.

Interlude 2

G | | | D |
(Oh.   Oh.

Em | | | |Cadd9
Oh.   Oh.   Oh.

| |D |N.C. |G |
Oh.   Oh.   Oh, oh.)   This is me. (Oh.)

Bridge

‖G | D |Em |
And I know that I de - serve your ___ love.

| | |C | |Dsus4 |
There's nothing I'm not worthy of.

Chorus 3

‖G | | |
When the sharpest words wanna cut me down,

|Em7 | | |
I'm gonna send a flood, gonna drown 'em out.

|Cadd9 |
This is brave,   this is bruised.

|Dsus4 |N.C.
This is who ___ I'm meant to be.

|G   N.C.
This is me.

G | | |
   Look out, 'cause here I come;

|Em7 | | |
And I'm marchin' on to the beat I drum.

|Cadd9 | |Dsus4 |N.C.
I'm not scared   to be seen. I make no ___ apologies.

This is me.

Outro

‖G |
(When - ever the words wanna cut me down,

| | D |Em | | |
I'll send the flood to drown them ___ out.

D |Cadd9 | |D |N.C.(G)
Oh. ___   Oh.   Oh.   Oh, oh.)

‖
This is me.

Rewrite the Stars

Words and Music by
Benj Pasek and Justin Paul

(Capo 3rd fret)

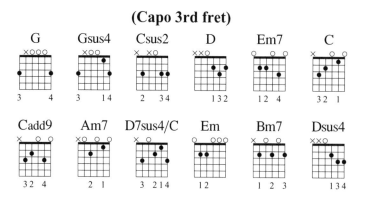

Verse 1

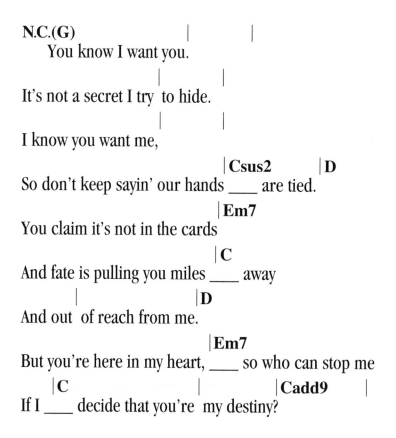

N.C.(G) | |
   You know I want you.

| |
It's not a secret I try to hide.

| |
I know you want me,

|**Csus2** |**D**
So don't keep sayin' our hands ___ are tied.

|**Em7**
You claim it's not in the cards

|**C**
And fate is pulling you miles ___ away

| |**D**
And out of reach from me.

|**Em7**
But you're here in my heart, ___ so who can stop me

|**C** | |**Cadd9** |
If I ___ decide that you're my destiny?

Chorus 1

‖ **Em7** |**C**
What if we   rewrite the stars?

               |**G** |**D**
Say you were made ____ to be mine.

         |**Em7** |**C**
Nothing could keep us apart;

            |**G** |**D**
You'd be the one ____ I was meant to find.

         |**Em7** |**C**
It's up to you, ____ and it's up to me.

           |**G** |**D**
No one can say ____ what we get to be.

          |**Em7** |**C**
So why don't we rewrite the stars?

           |**G** |**D**   ‖
Maybe the world ____ could be ours ____ tonight?

Interlude 1 |**G** |**Am7** |**Em7** |**D**   ‖

Verse 2

G |**Gsus4** |**G**
     You think it's easy?

                   |**Gsus4** |**G**
You think I don't want to run ____ to you?

               |**Gsus4** |**G**
But there are mountains

                  |**Gsus4** |**D**
And there are doors that we can't ____ walk through.

            |**Em7** |**C**
I know you're wondering why, ____ because we're able to be

        | |**D**
Just you and me   within these   walls.

            |**Em7**
But when we go outside, ____ you're gonna wake up

       |**C** | |**D7sus4/C** |
And see ____ that it was hope - less after all.

Chorus 2

     ‖**Em7** |**C**
No one can rewrite the stars?

        |**G** |**D**
How can you say ____ you'll be mine?

      |**Em7** |**C**
Ev'rything keeps us apart;

         |**G** |**D**
And I'm not the one ____ you were meant to find.

       |**Em7** |**C**
It's not up to you. ____ It's not up to me,

       |**G** |**D**
When ev'ryone tells ____ us what we can be.

      |**Em7** |**C**
How can we rewrite the stars?

        |**G** |**D**   ‖
Say that the world ____ can be ours ____ tonight?

Bridge

Em |**C** |**G**
  All I want is to fly ____ with you.

        |**D** |**Em**
All I want is to fall ____ with you.

       |**Bm7** |**C**
So just give me all ____ of you.

     |**Cadd9** |
It feels im - possible.   Is it im - possible?
      (It's not impossible.)

     | | **N.C.**
 Say that it's possible.

Chorus 3

‖**Em7** |**C**
How do we rewrite the stars?

        |**G** |**D**
Say you were made ___ to be mine.

  |**Em7** |**C**
Nothing can keep us apart;

        |**G** |**D**
'Cause you are the one ___ I was meant to find.

   |**Em7** |**C**
It's up to you, ___ and it's up to me.

    |**G** |**D**
No one can say ___ what we get to be.

   |**Em7** |**C**
So why don't we rewrite the stars?

      |**G** |**D**   ‖
Changing the world ___ to be ours.

Interlude 2

|**G** |**Gsus4** |**G** |**Gsus4**   ‖

Outro-Verse

G |**Gsus4** |**G**
    You know I want you.

       |**Gsus4** |**G**
It's not a secret I try ___ to hide.

       |**Gsus4** |**G**
But I can't have you.

          |**N.C.**   ‖
We're bound to break and my hands are tied.

Tightrope

Words and Music by
Benj Pasek and Justin Paul

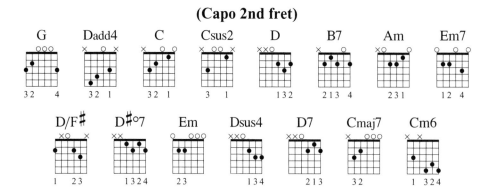

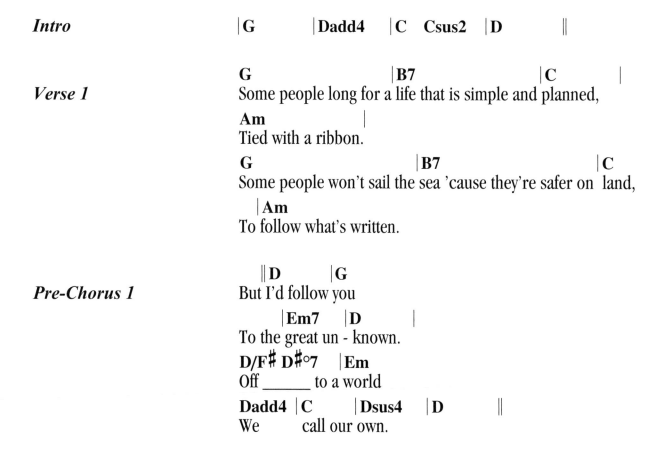

Intro
| G | Dadd4 | C   Csus2 | D   ‖

Verse 1

G | B7 | C |
Some people long for a life that is simple and planned,

Am |
Tied with a ribbon.

G | B7 | C
Some people won't sail the sea 'cause they're safer on land,

| Am
To follow what's written.

Pre-Chorus 1

‖ D | G
But I'd follow you

| Em7 | D |
To the great un - known.

D/F♯ D♯°7 | Em
Off _____ to a world

Dadd4 | C | Dsus4 | D   ‖
We   call our own.

Chorus 1

```
G                          |D7              |Em
```
Hand in my hand and we promise to never let go.
```
      |C                   |
```
We're walkin' a tightrope.
```
G                          |D7              |Em
```
High in the sky, we can see the whole world down be - low.
```
      |C            |Em
```
We're walkin' a tightrope.
```
      |C       |G             |Dsus4
```
Never sure, never know how far we could fall.
```
        |G              |D7            |Em   Dadd4  |
```
But it's all an adventure that comes with a breathtaking view;
```
C                |Cmaj7      ||
```
Walkin' a tightrope ___ with…

Interlude 1

```
N.C.(G) (Dadd4) |(Em)  (Dsus4) |(C)      |
```
You,   oo,   oo,   oo,   oo,
```
      |G   Dadd4 |Em  Dadd4  |
```
With you, oo,   oo, oo,
```
C       |D     ||
```
Oo, with you.

Verse 2

```
G                          |B7              |C        |
```
Mountains and valleys and all ___ that will come in be - tween;
```
Am             |
```
Desert and ocean.
```
G                 |B7           |C        |
```
You pull me in and to - gether we're lost in a dream,
```
Am
```
Always in motion.

Pre-Chorus 2

```
        ‖D      |G
So  I risk it all
        |Em7  |D
Just to be with you.
      |D/F♯ D♯°7    |Em   Dadd4
And I _____ risk it all
        |C      |Dsus4   D      ‖
For this life we choose.
```

Chorus 2

```
G                       |D7              |Em
Hand in my hand and you promised to never let go.
      |C                |
We're walkin' a tightrope.
G                 |D7                    |Em
High in the sky, we can see the whole world down be - low.
      |C              |Em
We're walkin' a tightrope.
      |C      |G              |Cm6    |N.C.
Never sure, will you  catch me if I should  fall.
      |G              |D7              |Em  Dadd4  |
Well, it's all an adventure that comes with a breathtaking view;
C              |Cmaj7      ‖
Walkin' a tightrope ___ with…
```

Outro

```
N.C.(G)  (Dadd4) |(Em)  (Dsus4)  |(C)      |
You,      oo,        oo,   oo,          oo.
      |G  Dadd4 |Em  Dadd4  |
With you oo,        oo,  oo,
C      |Dadd4 D  |G  B7  |Em   D    |
Oo, with you,
C      |Cm6      |  N.C.
With you,
      |G    D/F♯   |
With you,
Em    D   |C
      |D      |G          ‖
Oo,      with you.
```

From Now On

Words and Music by
Benj Pasek and Justin Paul

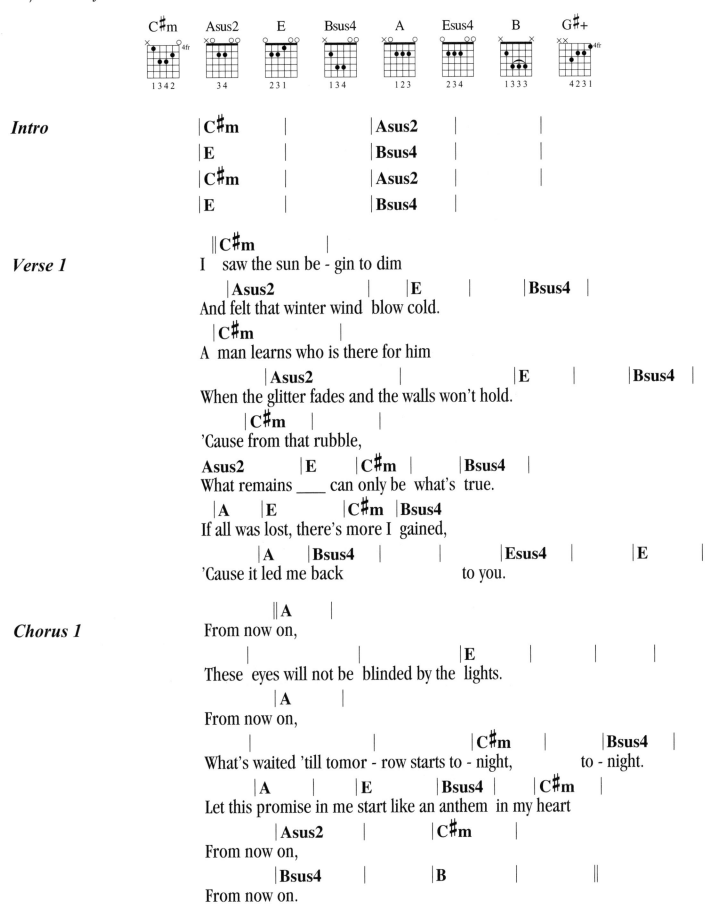

Intro

C#m		Asus2		
E		Bsus4		
C#m		Asus2		
E		Bsus4		

Verse 1

||C#m |
I   saw the sun be - gin to dim
    |Asus2 | |E | |Bsus4 |
And felt that winter wind blow cold.
    |C#m |
A man learns who is there for him
        |Asus2 | |E | |Bsus4 |
When the glitter fades and the walls won't hold.
        |C#m | |
'Cause from that rubble,
Asus2 |E |C#m | |Bsus4 |
What remains ___ can only be what's true.
    |A |E |C#m |Bsus4
If all was lost, there's more I gained,
        |A |Bsus4 | | |Esus4 | |E |
'Cause it led me back   to you.

Chorus 1

        ||A |
From now on,
    | | |E | | |
These eyes will not be blinded by the lights.
        |A |
From now on,
    | | |C#m | |Bsus4 |
What's waited 'till tomor - row starts to - night,   to - night.
        |A | |E |Bsus4 | |C#m |
Let this promise in me start like an anthem in my heart
        |Asus2 | |C#m |
From now on,
        |Bsus4 | |B | | ||
From now on.

Interlude
```
|C♯m        |            |Asus2     |              |
|E          |            |Bsus4     |          |          |
```

Verse 2
```
  ‖C♯m                    |
I  drank champagne with kings and queens,
  |Asus2     |          |E        |        |Bsus4   |
The politicians praised my ___ name.
  |C♯m                   |
But those were someone else's dreams,
  |Asus2     |          |E        |        |Bsus4   |
The pitfalls of the man I be - came.
  |C♯m       |          |Asus2           |E
For years and  years I chased their cheers,
 |C♯m              |              |Bsus4    |
A crazy speed of al - ways needing ___ more.
  |A      |E       |G♯+         |C♯m
But when I stop and ___ see you here,
  |A           |Bsus4    |Esus4   |          |E
I re - member who all this was ___ for.
```

Chorus 2
```
      |              ‖A        |
   And from now on,
    |              |          |E        |          |          |
These  eyes will not be  blinded by ___ the lights.
         |A        |
From now on,
      |              |              |C♯m      |           |Bsus4
What's waited 'till tomor - row starts ___ tonight.  It starts to - night.
       |     |A      |     |E  |       |Bsus4  |     |C♯m    |
And let this promise in me start like an anthem  in my heart
            |A           |          |C♯m      |
From now on,
           |Bsus4     |          |          |
From now ___ on,
                 ‖
From now on.
```

Bridge 1

‖:C♯m | |Asus2
      And we will come back home,

          | |E |
And we will come back home,

      |Bsus4 | :‖
Home again.

C♯m | |Asus2
      And we will come back home,

         | |E |
And we will come back home,

      |Bsus4 |
Home again.

      |C♯m
From now on.

      | |Asus2
And we will come back home,

        | |E |
And we will come back home,

      |Bsus4 | |
Home again.

N.C.(C♯m) | |(Asus2)
      And we will come back home,

        | |(E) |
And we will come back home. Yes!

      |(Bsus4) | |
Home again.

(C♯m) | |(Asus2)
      And we will come back home,

        | |(E) |
And we will come back home,

      |(Bsus4) |
Home again.

Chorus 3

N.C.   ‖**A** |
From now on,

     | | |**E** | | |
These eyes will not be blinded by ___ the lights.

      |**A** |
From now on,

     | | |**C♯m** |
What's waited 'till tomor - row starts ___ tonight,

    |**Bsus4** | |
It starts ___ tonight.

     |**A** | **E** |**Bsus4** | **C♯m** |
Let this promise in me start like an anthem in my heart

    |**Asus2** | **C♯m** |
From now on,

    |**Bsus4** | **B** |
From now on,

    ‖
From now…

Bridge 2

C♯m | |Asus2
    And we will come back home,
On.

   | |E |
And we will come back home,

  |Bsus4 |
Home again.

    |C♯m
From now on.

   | |Asus2
And we will come back home,

   | |E |
And we will come back home,

  |Bsus4 ‖
Home again.

‖:C♯m | |Asus2
    And we will come back home,

   | |E |
And we will come back home,

  |Bsus4 | :‖
Home again.

C♯m |

   |Asus2 |
From now on,

  |E |
From now on.

  |Bsus4 | |
Home a - gain.

C♯m | |Asus2 |
Oo,   from now on,

  |E |
From now on.

  |Bsus4 | | ‖
Home a - gain.

STRUM & SING

Lyrics, chord symbols, and guitar chord diagrams for your favorite songs.

GUITAR

ADELE
00159855......................$12.99

SARA BAREILLES
00102354......................$12.99

BLUES
00159335......................$12.99

ZAC BROWN BAND
02501620......................$12.99

COLBIE CAILLAT
02501725......................$14.99

CAMPFIRE FOLK SONGS
02500686......................$12.99

CHART HITS OF 2014-2015
00142554......................$12.99

CHART HITS OF 2015-2016
00156248......................$12.99

BEST OF KENNY CHESNEY
00142457......................$14.99

KELLY CLARKSON
00146384......................$14.99

JOHN DENVER COLLECTION
02500632......................$9.95

EAGLES
00157994......................$12.99

EASY ACOUSTIC SONGS
00125478......................$14.99

50 CHILDREN'S SONGS
02500825......................$8.99

THE 5 CHORD SONGBOOK
02501718......................$12.99

FOLK SONGS
02501482......................$10.99

FOLK/ROCK FAVORITES
02501669......................$10.99

THE 4 CHORD SONGBOOK
02501533......................$12.99

THE 4-CHORD COUNTRY SONGBOOK
00114936......................$14.99

HAMILTON
00217116......................$14.99

HITS OF THE '60S
02501138......................$12.99

HITS OF THE '70S
02500871......................$9.99

HYMNS
02501125......................$8.99

JACK JOHNSON
02500858......................$16.99

ROBERT JOHNSON
00191890......................$12.99

CAROLE KING
00115243......................$10.99

BEST OF GORDON LIGHTFOOT
00139393......................$14.99

DAVE MATTHEWS BAND
02501078......................$10.95

JOHN MAYER
02501636......................$10.99

INGRID MICHAELSON
02501634......................$10.99

THE MOST REQUESTED SONGS
02501748......................$12.99

JASON MRAZ
02501452......................$14.99

PRAISE & WORSHIP
00152381......................$12.99

ELVIS PRESLEY
00198890......................$12.99

QUEEN
00218578......................$12.99

ROCK AROUND THE CLOCK
00103625......................$12.99

ROCK BALLADS
02500872......................$9.95

ED SHEERAN
00152016......................$14.99

THE 6 CHORD SONGBOOK
02502277......................$10.99

CAT STEVENS
00116827......................$14.99

TAYLOR SWIFT
00159856......................$12.99

THE 3 CHORD SONGBOOK
00211634......................$9.99

TODAY'S HITS
00119301......................$12.99

TOP CHRISTIAN HITS
00156331......................$12.99

KEITH URBAN
00118558......................$14.99

NEIL YOUNG – GREATEST HITS
00138270......................$14.99

UKULELE

THE BEATLES
00233899......................$16.99

COLBIE CAILLAT
02501731......................$10.99

JOHN DENVER
02501694......................$10.99

FOLK ROCK FAVORITES FOR UKULELE
00114600......................$9.99

THE 4-CHORD UKULELE SONGBOOK
00114331......................$14.99

JACK JOHNSON
02501702......................$17.99

JOHN MAYER
02501706......................$10.99

INGRID MICHAELSON
02501741......................$12.99

THE MOST REQUESTED SONGS
02501453......................$14.99

JASON MRAZ
02501753......................$14.99

SING-ALONG SONGS
02501710......................$15.99

HAL•LEONARD®

www.halleonard.com
Visit our website to see full song lists.